DATE DUE

Metro Litho
Oak Forest, IL 60452

MAR 10. 1993	JUL 25. 1994	NOV 05 '03	JUN 1 8 '08
JUN. 12. 1993	SEP 02. 1994	JAN 27 '04	
JUL. 13. 1993	MAR 01. 1995		DEC 0 8 '08
AUG. 10. 1993	JUL 07. 1995	FEB 01 '05	
OCT. 28. 1993	APR. 01. 1996	JUL 0 9 '05	
JAN. 04. 1994	DEC. 11. 1996	MAR 1 8 '06	
FEB. 28. 1994	JUN. 25. 1997	JUL 2 7 '06	
APR. 21. 1994	APR. 06. 1999	NOV 1 3 '06	
MAY 17. 1994	SEP. 16. 1999	APR 2 6 '07	
JUN. 20. 1994	MAR 07. 2000	MAY 1 6 '07	
	AUG. 07. 2000	JUN 1 9 '07	
JUL. 14. 1994	MAY 21 '02		

12.95   119892

2629-7

636.3   Potter, Tessa
POT   Goats

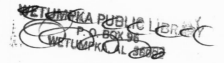

Animal World

Goats

Tessa Potter and Donna Bailey

STECK-VAUGHN
LIBRARY
A Division of Steck-Vaughn Company

This farmer has goats on her farm.
She keeps the goats for their milk.

The goats eat the grass
in the field.
They eat the weeds, too.

The goats like to eat leaves and
twigs.
The food keeps the goats healthy.

The farmer puts her goats on a leash.
She takes them for a walk.
The goats can eat twigs from the hedges.

Sometimes the farmer cuts some branches.
She hangs them in the goat stall
for the goats to eat.

The goats sleep in the goat stall
when it is cold.

The farmer takes care of her goats.
She gives them fresh water to drink.

Their hooves grow quickly.
Every month a man cuts their hooves.
It does not hurt the goats.

9

One of the goats is a male goat.

He is called a billy goat.

He has a long beard.

The female goats are called nanny goats.
This nanny goat has mated with
the billy goat.
She will soon have babies.

A baby goat is called a kid.
This kid is drinking its mother's milk.

After five days, the farmer teaches
the kids to drink milk from a bucket.
They each suck the milk up through a tube.

Now the farmer can have
the goat's milk.
She takes the goat to the milking stand.

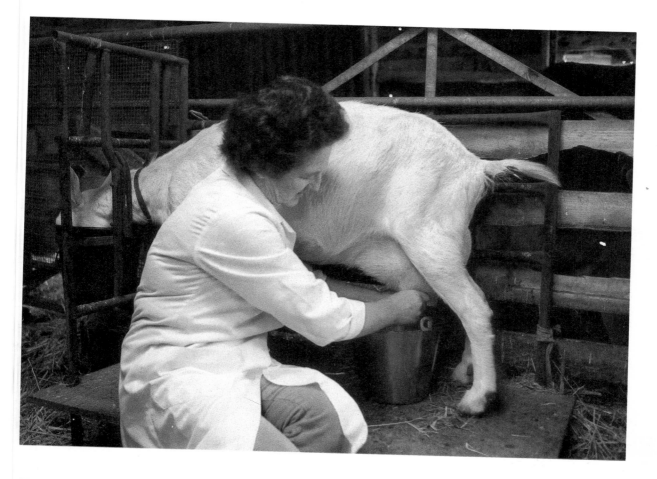

The farmer milks her goats twice a day.
She squeezes the goat's udder gently.
The milk goes into a bucket.
The farmer likes to drink goat's milk.

The farmer uses some of the milk to make
cheese and yogurt.
Goats are important to people.
They eat weeds and give us milk.

16

Goats lives in different parts
of the world.
Some goats live in mountains, some
live in deserts.
They do not need good grass to eat.

There are many different kinds of goats.
This mohair goat has long hair.
People use the hair to make a soft cloth.

18

These people live in the desert.
They move around the desert with
their herds of goats.

These goats climb trees to eat the leaves.

They eat the rough desert grass.

People who live in the desert often use goatskins to carry water from the well.

They live in black tents that
they make from goat hair.

The women take care of the goats
and milk them.

If a goat won't stand still,
one of the girls finds a kid.

She shows the kid to the goat.
Then the goat will stand still.

These are wild goats.

They live in high mountains.

They have very big horns.

Goats are good at climbing.
This wild goat is climbing over
the rocks to look for food.

These are tame goats.
In the summer they live
in the mountains.
They eat the grass and leaves in
the mountain fields.

In the winter the farmer brings
the goats down from the mountains.
They stay in a warm shed.
The farmer gives them hay to eat.

The farmer milks his goats.
He sells some of the milk to
a chocolate factory.

He sells the rest of his milk
to a dairy where they make
different kinds of goat cheese.
People in many countries like goat cheese.

Index

billy goat 10, 11

chocolate 31

climbing 21, 28

cloth 18

desert 17, 19, 20, 21, 22, 23,
    24, 25

food 3, 4, 5, 6, 20, 21, 28, 29, 30

goat stall 6, 7

goatskin 22

hair 18, 23

hooves 9

horns 27

kid 12, 13, 25, 26

mating 11

milk 2, 12, 13, 14, 15, 16

milking 14, 15, 24, 25, 26, 31

mohair goat 18

mountains 17, 27, 28, 29, 30

nanny goat 11

shed 30

sleeping 7

tame goats 13

tents 23

udder 15

walks 5

water 8, 22

wild goats 27, 28

Reading Consultant: Diana Bentley
Editorial Consultant: Donna Bailey
Supervising Editor: Kathleen Fitzgibbon

Illustrated by Gill Tomblin
Picture research by Suzanne Williams
Designed by Richard Garratt Design

Photographs
Cover: Frank Lane Picture Agency/M. J. Thomas
Bruce Coleman: 18 (Hans Reinhard)
Frank Lane Picture Agency: 17 (W. Wisniewski) and 27 (Silvestris)
Peter Greenland: 1, 4, 5, 6, 7, 8, 9, 10, 11, 12, 13, 14, 15 and 16
Robert Harding Associates: 23, 24, 25 and 26
Eric and David Hosking: 22
Swiss National Tourist Board: 32
ZEFA: 19, 20, 21, 28 and 29

Note to the reader:
The goats illustrated on page 17 are from Namibia, page 19—
    Jerusalem, page 21 - Morocco, page 22 - Jordan, pages 23, 24, 25 and 26 -
    Iran, and page 28 - Italy.

Library of Congress Cataloging-in-Publication Data: Potter, Tessa. Goats/Tessa Potter and Donna Bailey; [illustrated by Gi Tomblin]. p. cm.—(Animal world) SUMMARY: Discusses the care and usefulness of goats on farms, in the desert, and in the mountains. ISBN 0-8114-2629-7 1. Goats—Juvenile literature. [1. Goats.] I. Bailey, Donna. II. Tomblin, Gill, ill. III. Title. IV. Series: Animal world (Austin, Tex.) SF383.35.P67 1990 636.3′9—dc20 89-22021 CIP AC

1 2 3 4 5 6 7 8 9 LB 96 95 94 93 92 91 90